T0290386

A Picture-Feeling

A Picture-Feeling

Renee Gladman

ROOF BOOKS
New York

ISBN: 978-1-931824-15-6

Library of Congress Catalog Card Number 2005900314

Cover art by Porfirio DiDonna

 This book is made possible, in part, by the New York State Council on the Arts with the support of the Office of the Governor and the New York State Legislature.

Roof Books are published by
Segue Foundation
300 Bowery #2
New York, NY 10012
seguefoundation.com

Roof Books are distributed by
Small Press Distribution
1341 Seventh Street
Berkeley, CA. 94710-1403
Phone orders: 800-869-7553
spdbooks.org

for she who sleeps
and she who doesn't sleep
and she who passed as sleep
and V

and I did not wish myself absent
for I did not know myself that way

—Hans Faverey

coming out of a dream whose content escapes me into a space
where V is in danger and where lies the knowledge that we are all
full of diasporic shapes that have no memory

Codes—

The iron twists
before they
      and before they
'feeling attached to ideas'
—form—
for the spectator
                  —need—
but soon dissolve
to rid the spectator
               this memory

though before that
made an imprint   that need

      then became pieces
      then everything

the iron twists
are meant   wrought iron
is the update
but not fixed
just now   'wrought iron'

        though once hypnosis
        failure becomes
        bits of paper
        in vastly empty—
        outside of box—

wrought *irons*, I should say

but to come away empty
as if there were no depth
as if never was
even though you're told

         'you've traveled'   rust
                            a contrived memory

      now placed
      beside the box

conveyor   of the dream

the books applied to the rust
the dream, the books
she will use to reach me
work from over there

but here
there is no such
                    accumulation
the rust is still the rust
and wrought irons
without a proven name
weigh out the rest
                        this room

and I haven't found
enough of box
to say 'box' again
so, just the large room

the wrought irons (not confirmed)
appeared inscrutably
at first
but before that   a dream
I wanted
not to see

to see V pressed
beneath a weight
terrible
(vast room later on?)
though usual
in her
content

but
pressed
and soon
not to breathe?

the dream completed itself
but the fear of loss held
then became
iron twisted
(which I still can't name
and it's the fourth day)
coming out   of the feeling

                        fear

the dream-head swollen
and called out

'Is V all right?'

she sleeps   How does one get an answer

I said, 'Is V all right'   then
the twists came   that is
the…(still)   they came

as a sculpture first
as a…

odd to come after waking
and even after speech
when space is less
                    liminal
when time is defined
as 'between'
because now
a part of the narrative:

                'What happened today'

instead of something
purely meaningful

                    dream

configured metal   a cast iron
sculpture
called 'feeling attached to ideas'
what matters here
the hardest to name
but takes up the most space
as any ignorance does
also the fear
that what you see
gets you
and V!
crushed though happy
not at all in space

that the 'feeling attached
to ideas' rushed in
after speech and
made the sudden flood
of sensation   foreboding
(it blared
as if lit from every corner)
does not mean
it captured anything

half-life, then
said now so it
doesn't show later   should have said
'wrought iron' before
I went to sleep that night
should say 'New York 2005'
to avoid that too
'early death' while we're at it

but maybe 'half-life'
represented by the vast room
means sitting in it
not *being* it
because   who could remove
such room
from self

how would
—to speak of hurricanes—
would they without Christian names
say 'feeling attached to flying things'   ?
houses flying   life-blown
and newscasters
pulling jackets closed
over Charley or Gus or Frances
my wrought irons
destroyed

the analogy fails
the iron twists   and the people
of Florida

the session with the hypnotist
an on-time arrival
this morning
making one
out of two
half languages
her half   mine
getting to
the body up
this morning

the analogy fails
the vast room
it neither gives nor robs
life   life-blown

without it   there is still
the box
torn bits of paper   and
the two   most impossible to reach
entering the room

none of this reality

to bring it to reality
requires encryption
        it's vastly cold here

here
bring the dream into reality
inside the hypnotist's door
        dream rendering
vast and forlorn

reality refusing the pieces
of iron-become-paper
just inside the door

                emptying out
                the dream

the iron twists
meet cast iron   in this
site of the unknown
on the seventh day
configuring beneath
a blank placard
that we are full
of 'pieces that don't know
themselves'
has yet to become newsworthy
—I have conveyed
the fact to four people

no precipitation

also no one yet
to name
the configuration
of 'wrought iron' as it weighs
in design culture

has to be something   known
attached to commerce

way we look at a plate
of glass
quartered by wood
and call it
        window

whatever (it is)   did not rise
out of the ordinary
so even if I named it
wouldn't be   that thing
still the shape that broke
apart and dropped a piece
in me   piece that
upon contact forgot name,
purpose, face
knew only those around it
as selfsame
is vivid
is blackness

—was surrendered for what
in this case   a message:
the flood of a feeling

      picture

              which
one convinced oneself
contained a truer message
though
          as with any flood
was washed away
         all meaning

it will surprise
if everything doesn't rust
if the fabrication
doesn't become
the thing
        the rust, the only quality to touch

is going to give us
wherewithal and then

she won't worry about me

the rust is better
than the books
because
you only have to see
rust

you don't need to read it

as I begin to lose them
the codes, the fakes,
the wrought irons
nameless   still nameless
on the eleventh day
and wonder in
this 'extent of a tragic
dream'
          as I begin to await
trains once again
leaving the 'feeling attached
to ideas' to the process
—memory—
of having written
codes   but not the codes
themselves
and still more

only after the fabrication
of hypnosis—that made up room—
was there a need to contrive

        I have mentioned the impossibility
        of the room—

                vast   imaginary

        in many

        but have I separated it
        from the rust   appropriately

not hypnosis failure, which
gave color   but time
however unrecoverable

from the room
the express train
widens the dispersal
of torn pieces of iron
now paper
the box holds mysteriously
having never been
deciphered the box
box is   we call the box

'what's waiting for me'

September 11 NYC
another 'wrought iron'
unexplained flooding
but 'what happened today'
a narrative to which
the state reacted badly
now commemorating

but every analogy

fails the   too personal

from each end   ends

with a dispute

over the middle

which is real   as seen

in flashes

rust reality or rust fantasy

wrought   iron or irons

the multiplicity

fails the analogue

because it's not just '9/11'

it's Venezuela

the Sudan

pre rust the iron
twists were dull
and new just
about to pull apart
just as I was flooded
with picture-feeling
—attached to ideas—
except this one
which was nameless (V
pinned beneath
unbearable weight)
or was
the moment before
the real thing and
V underneath—
the verb not
the subject

V—
pressed though content
—as V always is—
doesn't mind the weight

I would like to show her these
(wrought irons)
               what to do with them?

instead of contriving rust

               which has failed to become any
               one thing

a vertical flat
pressing upon V
with an orange light
coming through   enveloping
actually   the atmosphere
the space exposed
and more importantly
the unbearable
not yet dropped but
acting as if supposed to

the wrought irons
that are 'just that'—she says—
(and I still can't believe)
have become
'home' today
but tomorrow   another thing

because   who could repeat that losing

though it's not V
we've lost
from home

life has become desolate
since the wrought irons
fractionated and became
paper strewn
around the unnamed
box   absolutely desolate
when the piece I chose to
follow became
a near asphyxiated V
(though smiling)
and the light went out completely
when I put the two together
thought the word 'home'

On the fifty-first day
'wrought iron' confirmed
no need to qualify it
—people—
—things—
but speak of it
as it appears
proven:

form of
wrought irons
and content
'wrought iron'

                the selfsame

—but days after
      equalization

      what has happened to
      the 'pieces that
            don't know themselves'
about which

      she says,

          your memory saves you

      to not-remember
      the desolate
      feeling

         she means

the pieces
still progressing
the flying   things

progressing but not
        as ideas

but forms
of attachment

     —V would say—

or to get to the next place

where my piece
finds yours

     but if everything
     is flying   ?

you don't know yourself
        Nathalie Sarraute

who is not
that   really
more like

       Natasha and
whatever Russian
before taking   his name

as when I was never
           Annette

     and loved
        Francesca

the pieces, then
        the pieces

of iron (near exploding)
soundlessly

calls 'them' together

        but once they're
            gathered

obscures the convent
        we don't see our shape

some have the word
        'pieces'
            remaining

but it's a torn ticket

—where does it go—
—V do you have yourn—

clear that we don't
know ourselves today

       it's gray
       cold

and clear that

there will be   no reach

today
       vast room

in which each corner
holds   a question
a masked person
sound of scurrying

though not-human
scurry
       masked persons

thinking it's

       vast and cold
       and gray today

masked persons thinking

      the other more masked
      than herself

            thinking

                  gray cold today

how we made it thus

without answers

           or pictures

how it is enough
just to ask for them

            to pose as if waiting
                to wait
                     for them

a sign reads 'you have plenty'
but how do you expect to see it   here

      there are no lights on
      'They' won't let you pull
      this shade

so this is   the shade
of de-rusting

this is the clear black

shade

       the vivid
       black
       unseeing

the forgetting obscurity
       making codes
               'pieces that'

of 'the two most
impossible to reach'

      the one dead
      worries me
      less
      to the foreign one

      who's nearing the point
                    moment of obscurity
                    entrance into the poem

it ruins
to give people-names
more power
than axes
      of time and space

the one who sleeps puzzles   Chicago

foreign one   step over
put this around
      your shoulders

put this

        on your head

        foreign one
        sleep now

        against the imprint
        of culture   my
        writing onto yours
        mine
        selfsame
        retardant

foreign   uncontrived
one, you wrought iron

V doesn't know you

wrought iron transom

      dream to vast room

the rusting century-
old walkway

ghosts   I've invited
along the transom

      and non-
        ghosts who

pass the walkway
searching   the room

            entrance is impossible

except for the hypnotist
the sleeper
    who enters

enters   the afterthought
of structure

      provides the trance
      for crossing
      invitation for the unknown

though it never showed
though it was paper

codes appropriately
exercised

      said 'bye-bye'

      days ago
      but hid the act
      —in sleep—

must be something
           'more upset,'
               she said

         where is your imprint

            wherein
            it pressed
            this life

      lightly

            to make
            mystery

to make need
      but never shape

'you should be'

they finished themselves

                              wake up
                              hypnotist

ROOF BOOKS
the best in language since 1976

Recent & Selected Titles

FOR TRAPPED THINGS by Brian Kim Stefans. 138 p. $20

EXCURSIVE by Elizabeth Robinson. 140 p. $20

I, BOOMBOX by Robert Glück. 194 p. $20

TRUE ACCOUNT OF TALKING TO THE 7 IN SUNNYSIDE
by Paolo Javier. 192 p. $20

THE NIGHT BEFORE THE DAY ON WHICH by Jean Day. 118 p. $20

MINE ECLOGUE by Jacob Kahn. 104 p. $20

SCISSORWORK by Uche Nduka. 150 p. $20

DOG DAY ECONOMY by Ted Rees. 138 p. $20

THIEF OF HEARTS by Maxwell Owen Clark. 116 p. $20

QUANUNDRUM: [i will be your many angled thing]
by Edwin Torres, 128 p. $20

THE NERVE EPISTLE by Sarah Riggs. 106 p. $20

FETAL POSITION by Holly Melgard. 110 p. $20

DEATH & DISASTER SERIES by Lonely Christopher. 192 p. $20

BIONIC COMMUNALITY by Brenda Iijima. 150 p. $20

URBAN POETRY FROM CHINA editors Huang Fan and
James Sherry, translation editor Daniel Tay. 412 p. $25

BIONIC COMMUNALITY by Brenda Iijima. 150 p. $20

THE COMBUSTION CYCLE by Will Alexande. 614 p. $25

QUEENZENGLISH.MP3: POETRY: POETRY, PHILOSOPHY,
PERFORMATIVITY, Edited by Kyoo Lee. 176 p. $20

MIRROR MAGIC by John Sakkis. 96 p. $18.95

UNSOLVED MYSTERIES by Marie Buck. 96 p. $18.95

I AM, AM I TO TRUST THE JOY THAT JOY IS NO MORE OR
LESS THERE NOW THAN BEFORE by Evan Kennedy. 82 p. $18.95

THE COURSE by Ted Greenwald & Charles Bernstein. 250 p. $20

PLAIN SIGHT by Steven Seidenberg. 216 p. $19.95

IN A JANUARY WOULD by Lonely Christopher, 90 p. $17.95

POST CLASSIC by erica kaufman. 96 p. $16.95
JACK AND JILL IN TROY by Bob Perelman, 96 p. $16.95
UN\\MARTYRED: [SELF-]VANISHING PRESENCES
IN VIETNAMESE POETRY by Nha Thuyen. 174 p. $17.95
MOSTLY CLEARING by Michael Gottlieb, 112 p. $17.95
THE RIOT GRRRL THING by Sara Larsen, 112 p. $16.95
THOUGHT BALLOON by Kit Robinson, 104p. $16.95

Roof Books are published by
Segue Foundation
300 Bowery #2 • New York, NY 10012
seguefoundation.com

Roof Books are distributed by
SMALL PRESS DISTRIBUTION
1341 Seventh Street • Berkeley, CA. 94710-1403.
spdbooks.org

Made in the USA
Middletown, DE
23 May 2023

30854964R00050